# DANGEROUS DINOSAURS

Written by Carey Scott
Consultant David Lambert

DK

LONDON, NEW YORK,
MELBOURNE, MUNICH, AND DELHI

**Senior Art Editor**  Smiljka Surla
**Senior Editor**  Fran Jones
**Managing Editor**  Linda Esposito
**Managing Art Editor**  Diane Thistlethwaite
**Publishing Manager**  Andrew Macintyre
**Category Publisher**  Laura Buller
**Design Development Manager**  Sophia M. Tampakopoulos
**Production Editor**  Hitesh Patel
**DK Picture Library**  Claire Bowers
**Jacket Editor**  Mariza O'Keeffe
**Jacket Designers**  Sophia M. Tampakopoulos,
Natasha Rees

First published in the United States in 2008
by DK Publishing
375 Hudson Street, New York, New York 10014

A catalog record for this book is available
from the Library of Congress.

ISBN 978-0-7566-3502-2

Printed and bound in China by Hung Hing

Find out more at
**www.dk.com**

# CONTENTS

# AGE OF THE DINOSAURS

# What is a dinosaur?

Dinosaurs were land-dwelling reptiles with long tails, clawed hands and feet, and scaly skin. Some walked on two legs, others on four. While some were meat-eaters, others munched on plants. Most people know what a dinosaur looks like from books and movies. But even experts are still unsure why dinosaurs survived when their rivals died out. It was probably their erect stance, the sheer size of the largest, such as *Giganotosaurus,* and their efficient weapons of attack and defense that ensured their long-lasting success.

Long tail used for balance

Many dinosaurs had scaly skin covered with bumps

*Giganotosaurus*

**Q** **A** **In what way were dinosaurs different?**
Dinosaurs were different from other reptiles because they could stand with their legs straight. Most reptiles have legs that splay out from their bodies, giving them a sprawling stance. Dinosaurs were like mammals—they could walk upright with their legs directly below them.

Semisprawling stance of a crocodile | Sprawling stance of a lizard | Erect stance of a *Barosaurus*

Legs held straight beneath body

*Barosaurus*

**Q** **A** **Was *Eoraptor* the first of the dinosaurs?**
It was certainly one of the earliest dinosaurs. The remains of *Eoraptor*— a small, meat-eating dinosaur—were discovered in 1991 in South America, where dinosaurs may have originated. Experts estimate that *Eoraptor* was alive and well as long as 228 million years ago.

Five-fingered hands with weaker claws than later species

Powerful back legs

Some dinosaurs had a backward pointing toe

*Eoraptor*

Large, clawed, birdlike feet

Nostril

Serrated teeth for
tearing flesh

Powerful jaw

Most meat-eaters
had three
clawed fingers
on each hand

Bones of
Tyrannosaurus
foot

 **Did dinosaurs
have claws?**
All dinosaurs had clawed feet and
hands. Some claws were like the talons of
birds of prey, while others resembled
curved, sharp scissors. They were either
used to hook high branches down for food
or to slash live prey or stab at attackers.
Some "claws" were more like the hooves of
cattle and merely acted to protect the toes.

*Rhamphorhynchus*

**Were there dinosaurs
that could fly?**
Dinosaurs were all land-dwelling
animals. But there were plenty of flying
creatures in the prehistoric skies, and
they were reptiles, just like the dinosaurs.
They were called pterosaurs, which
means "winged lizard." There were many
different types of pterosaur, some as big
as light aircraft. *Rhamphorhynchus* was over
3 ft (1 m) long with a narrow jaw and
pointed teeth for catching fish.

Wing
membrane

# More Facts

■ The word dinosaur means "terrible
lizard" and was first used in 1842.

■ Dinosaurs and pterosaurs evolved from
a group of reptiles called archosaurs,
which arose 250 million years ago.

■ *Chasmatosaurus* was one of the
earliest archosaurs. It probably spent
most of its time hunting fish in rivers,
much like a modern crocodile.

*Chasmatosaurus*

**Were dinosaurs
warm-blooded?**
No one is sure. Reptiles such as
snakes are cold-blooded, which means
that their body temperature cools down
with the outside temperature and they
become less active. But evidence suggests
that some dinosaurs, such as *Velociraptor*,
had feathers, and feathered animals are
warm-blooded. Some experts now
believe that all the dinosaurs may have
been warm-blooded, enabling them
to be active whatever the weather.

*Velociraptor*

# How do we know about them?

Everything we know about dinosaurs comes from scientific evidence. That means the real, physical remains of the animals that have been preserved in the world's deserts, riverbeds, and cliffs for millions and millions of years. It was not until the 19th century that the remains were correctly identified and the science of paleontology was born. Since then, amazing discoveries have been made worldwide, including this complete skeleton of *Coelophysis*, unearthed in the sands of Texas.

*Coelophysis*

Ammonite

The remains of this dinosaur's last meal— a lizardlike animal— are still in its stomach

### Q A What is a fossil?

A fossil is the preserved remains of a plant or animal. These remains can be either hardened bones, shells, or other parts, or a preserved impression of the hard parts. One of the most common fossils is an ammonite—a shelled sea creature that lived at the same time as the dinosaurs.

### Q A When were dinosaurs first identified?

People have been collecting dinosaur fossils for many years, but it was not until 1842 that dinosaurs were recognized as a distinct group of animals. When this jaw was found in England, experts realized that this, and other remains, belonged to extinct giant reptiles. Soon the term "dinosaur" was used to describe them.

*Megalosaurus jaw*

## How is a fossil formed?

Fossils are formed by a process called mineralization. A creature dies and its soft parts rot away, leaving the skeleton. Minerals from water seep into the bones. The minerals eventually solidify, turning the bones into stone. Dinosaur fossils are often found in riverbeds, where the bodies have been quickly covered in sand and mud.

**4** Surface erosion exposes the fossilized bones, which can then be excavated by fossil experts.

**2** The soft tissues rot away, but the skeleton of the dinosaur stays more or less intact.

**1** A dinosaur is chased into a slow-flowing river, where it drowns and sinks into the mud.

**3** Millions of years later the ancient landscape has been buried, and new types of animals have evolved.

Two rows of pointed plates along spine

Spiked tail

*Tuojiangosaurus*

The horns give this dinosaur its name

## Q | A How is a dinosaur skeleton made?

People often think that dinosaur skeletons in museums are real, but they are usually replicas. Paleontologists create a complete skeleton from synthetic bones, using a few fossilized bones and skeletons of dinosaur relatives as a guide. Some skeletons are made from a mix of fossilized and synthetic bones.

## Q | A What is a paleontologist?

Paleontologists are those scientists who study fossils. They work both at the world's fossil sites, excavating fossils, and in the laboratory, cleaning and analyzing fossils. Here, a paleontologist treats a sauropod bone before moving it from the Sahara Desert. Dinosaur bones are easily uncovered in the desert sands without the need to dig deep.

## Q | A How do dinosaurs get their names?

Many dinosaurs are named after a distinguishing feature. For example, *Triceratops* means "three-horned face." Some are named because of where they were found—*Argentinosaurus* is a "reptile of Argentina." Others are called after the person who discovered them: *Herrerasaurus* means "Herrera's reptile."

*Triceratops*

# How long did dinosaurs rule?

Dinosaurs stomped their way across the Earth for about 160 million years and were the dominant land animals for 143 million years. During this huge stretch of time (humans have been around for less than 2 million years), many species became extinct but others evolved to take their place. Dinosaurs were survivors and most were able to adapt to their ever-changing world. *Dilophosaurus*, although not the largest of dinosaurs, was a meat-eater from the Jurassic Period. The last dinosaur expired 65 million years ago.

*Plateosaurus*

## Q Why do species die out?

**A** All living things die, and all species eventually become extinct. Most individual species of dinosaur existed for about 2–3 million years. Some species evolved into different ones by adapting to changing habitats, while others were unable to adapt. Some, such as *Plateosaurus*, may have died out because of a violent change to the environment that wiped out many animals.

## Q Who ruled before the dinosaurs?

**A** Before the age of the dinosaurs, the land was dominated by a group of animals that were neither reptiles nor mammals. The therapsids included this *Lystrosaurus*, a stocky, tusked plant-eater, about the size of a sheep. Most were extinct by 200 million years ago, when the dinosaurs grew dominant, although no one knows if they were wiped out by the dinosaurs.

Pair of bony crests on head

*Dilophosaurus*

Muscular neck

Three claws on hand

*Lystrosaurus*

Long, slim legs and feet

## When did dinosaurs live?

Our planet Earth was probably formed about 4.5 billion years ago, and the first animal life appeared about 1 billion years ago. The age when dinosaurs lived (from 251–65 mya) is called the Mesozoic Era, and scientists divide this into three periods—Triassic, Jurassic, and Cretaceous.

**1** The first dinosaurs, such as Eoraptor and Herrerasaurus, appeared in the mid **Triassic Period.**

**2** The **Jurassic Period** was dominated by the giant plant-eaters. Plated dinosaurs, such as the stegosaurs, appeared then, too.

*Dilophosaurus*

*Stegosaurus*

Herrerasaurus

Lesothosaurus

Anchisaurus

251 million years ago (mya)  **TRIASSIC**          200 mya                          **JURASSIC**

Section of backbone

*Lump on the vertebra, possibly caused by cancer*

**Q A Did dinosaurs ever get sick?**

Since the main dinosaur evidence is their bones, the only diseases that experts have found are those that affect the bones. This section of a dinosaur's backbone shows a tumor that may have been caused by cancer. Although it cannot be scientifically proved, it is likely that dinosaurs suffered from infectious diseases, just as animals do today.

*Velociraptor attacking Protoceratops*

**Q A How many groups existed together?**

Many dinosaur species became extinct while new species evolved over the long period of dinosaur rule, so many species did not coexist. Even so, dozens or even hundreds of different species did live at the same time in the same area. Experts know that *Velociraptor* was around at the same time as *Protoceratops*, because fossilized bones of the two have been discovered locked in battle.

Model of *Baryonyx*

**Q A How long did a dinosaur usually live?**

Bigger animals usually have a longer lifespan than small ones, so it is likely that the big plant-eating dinosaurs lived the longest. If one of these had a lucky life, it may have survived for 200 years or more. However, most dinosaurs would have died from accidents, starvation, or illness long before they could reach old age.

*Small head*

*Very long neck*

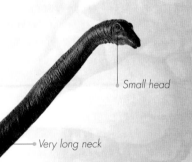

Archaeopteryx

Barosaurus

Baryonyx

Iguanodon

Deinonychus

**3** The dinosaurs were at their height in the **Cretaceous Period**. Some grew horns and frills, others developed club tails, and some refined their killing instincts.

Corythosaurus

Triceratops

Europlocephalus

145 mya    **CRETACEOUS**    65 mya

# Were all dinosaurs the same?

No, they were not. There were lumbering animals as big as buses. There were long-necked giants as tall as trees. There were massive predators that none could challenge. And darting around their feet were nimble chicken-sized dinosaurs. Some dinosaurs were numerous; others were rare. Some were plated, frilled, or horned; others were merely weird looking. *Chindesaurus*, shown here, was a carnivorous dinosaur that lived during the late Triassic Period. All the different dinosaurs belonged to one of two types.

Thick neck

Short arms for grasping prey

*Chindesaurus*

## What are the two main types of dinosaur?

The first dinosaurs evolved into two different types or orders, based on the shape of the hip bones. Ornithischians were bird-hipped and saurischians were lizard-hipped. The two orders gave rise to different families made up of genera. More than 540 different genera have been described so far.

1 The hips of ornithischians were characterized by a pair of bones (the pubis and ischium) that lay alongside each other and pointed backward.

Pubis

Ischium
Ornithischian

2 In saurischians, the pubis was larger and pointed downward and slightly forward, while the ischium extended backward.

Ischium — Pubis

Saurischian

Triassic Earth

Clawed feet

## Q A Which was the most common dinosaur?

Experts can only estimate the answer to this question based on the numbers of fossil finds. So many skulls of *Protoceratops* have been found in the Gobi Desert that the dinosaur is sometimes called the "sheep of the Gobi." In North America, the remains of entire herds of duck-billed or hadrosaur dinosaurs have been unearthed.

## Q A Where did dinosaurs live?

Dinosaurs lived in every part of the globe. However, when they first appeared, the world's land was a giant continent, known as Pangaea, which formed a C-shape around the Tethys Sea. Later, the landmass broke up into smaller continents. Dinosaur fossils have been found as far south as Antarctica, which was not covered with snow at that time.

Neck frill

*Protoceratops*

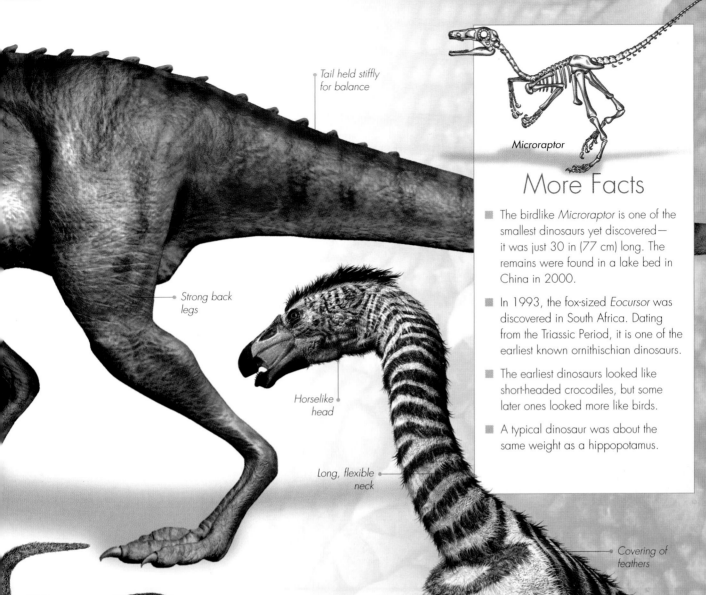

Tail held stiffly for balance

Microraptor

## More Facts

- The birdlike *Microraptor* is one of the smallest dinosaurs yet discovered—it was just 30 in (77 cm) long. The remains were found in a lake bed in China in 2000.

- In 1993, the fox-sized *Eocursor* was discovered in South Africa. Dating from the Triassic Period, it is one of the earliest known ornithischian dinosaurs.

- The earliest dinosaurs looked like short-headed crocodiles, but some later ones looked more like birds.

- A typical dinosaur was about the same weight as a hippopotamus.

Strong back legs

Horselike head

Long, flexible neck

Covering of feathers

Thick hair covered body

*Eozostrodon*

### Q A Were there any mammals?

Mammals evolved around the same time as the dinosaurs, so the two animal groups coexisted. But mammals were unable to compete with dinosaurs in size or ferocity and throughout the Mesozoic Era most were small, shrewlike animals. Many, like this *Eozostrodon*, hunted at night to avoid meat-eating dinosaurs. They fed on insects and other small animals.

### Q A Which was the weirdest dinosaur?

During the 1940s, paleontologists on fossil hunts in Mongolia made some unusual finds—giant claws over 3 ft (1 m) long, as well as parts of limbs. Some time later a skeleton was pieced together. What it revealed was a dinosaur like no other: two-legged, 36 ft (11 m) tall, with 8 ft- (2.5 m-) long arms ending in enormous claws, and probably covered with downy feathers. The weird find was named *Therizinosaurus*, meaning "scythe lizard."

*Therizinosaurus*

Clawed feet

# How was a dinosaur born?

Teeth and claws were not yet developed enough for the hatched baby to catch its own food

Dinosaurs did not give birth to live young in the way that mammals do. Like most reptiles, and like birds, female dinosaurs laid a number of eggs. These eggs were usually deposited in a nest made of twigs and leaves, or in a hole that the female had dug in the soil or sand. Dinosaur eggs could be oval or round and as small as a tennis ball or as large as a cannonball. A baby dinosaur, such as this *Troodon*, may have pecked its way out of its protective shell with a specially designed egg tooth, just as baby birds do.

*Troodon*

### Q A How many eggs did a dinosaur lay?

Some dinosaurs laid about 20 eggs and carefully arranged them in a circle inside the nest. Female sauropods may have laid up to 40 eggs. It is likely that dinosaurs laid eggs once a year, so a single female dinosaur probably hatched hundreds of babies in her lifetime. Experts think that between 50–90 percent of eggs survived to hatching.

Remains of discarded eggshells are common fossils found by nests

*Oviraptor*

18

## Q What was the biggest egg?

A Not surprisingly the biggest dinosaurs—the plant-eating sauropods—laid some of the biggest eggs, although these were surprisingly small. A sauropod egg weighed about 11 lb (5 kg) and was about 12 in (30 cm) long. This is only about twice the size of an ostrich egg, and tiny compared to the size of the mother.

*Troodon babies*

Sauropod eggs

## Q How fast did babies grow?

A After hatching, dinosaur babies, like these *Troodons*, grew quickly—most had to learn to defend themselves fast if they were to survive. Fossil evidence of hadrosaur young shows that they doubled in size in about six weeks. A one-year-old *Maiasaura* was about 10 ft (3 m) long. Depending on their type, dinosaurs were generally fully grown after about 14 years.

Colony of nesting gannets

## More Facts

■ Paleontologists think that some dinosaurs grew up in colonies, similar to those of modern nesting birds, such as gannets.

■ The sex of a dinosaur was determined by the temperature around the egg. If it was warm more males would hatch; a few degrees cooler and the babies would be mostly female.

■ Dinosaurs could be born as identical twins or even as triplets.

■ The largest known dinosaur egg is smaller than the egg of the extinct elephant bird of Madagascar.

## Q Did females sit on their nests?

A This 80 million-year-old fossilized *Oviraptor* nest proved to be an amazing discovery. The mother *Oviraptor* had died with her arms spread over her eggs, as if protecting them. This suggests that *Oviraptor*, and probably other birdlike dinosaurs, were brooders—they sat on their nests to keep the eggs warm or cool.

*Oviraptor on its nest*

*Eggs in nest*

## Q Did dinosaurs look after their young?

A Fossil evidence suggests that a female *Maiasaura* brought food to her babies after hatching, and may even have looked after her young for up to a year. There is no evidence that other dinosaurs cared for live young, but it is likely that many stayed near the nest to guard their eggs, like their closest living relatives, crocodiles.

Young *Maiasaura* with mother

# KILLERS AND SCAVENGERS

# What is a theropod?

Put simply, a theropod was a flesh-eating dinosaur. This lizard-hipped group of dinosaurs included some of the largest carnivores ever to roam the Earth. Although theropods often had wimpy arms, they did have strong muscles to power their rear legs. They also had large teeth and strong jaws. Most, such as *Carnotaurus*, had three-toed feet ending in claws. Not all theropods were huge—some were as small as chickens and survived by snapping up lizards and maybe insects.

*Tyrannosaurus clawed feet*

## Q A What does bipedal mean?

A bipedal animal is one that walks on two legs. All the meat-eating dinosaurs were bipedal, although there were some plant-eaters that also walked on two legs. Bipedal dinosaurs were faster and mostly more intelligent than their four-legged cousins. The first dinosaurs, such as *Eoraptor*, were bipedal, as were some of the later ones, such as *T. rex*.

*Large head*

*Muscular neck*

*Backbone*

*Small intestine*

*Megalosaurus tooth*

*Human tooth*

*Carnotaurus*

## Q A How big were a killer's teeth?

Carnivore fossils generally show curved, daggerlike teeth that would have sliced prey to shreds. The size of the tooth was generally a guide to the size of the animal and could be up to 8 in (20 cm) long. This tooth, which is 4 in (9 cm) long, comes from the mouth of *Megalosaurus*—a large theropod from the Jurassic Period.

*Short arms*

*Heart*

## How did a theropod run?

A dinosaur's fossilized bones and joints provide clues about how the animal moved. For example, paleontologists can figure out how far the limbs could reach. Large thigh bones indicate strong, muscular thighs, and long shin and foot bones suggest that the dinosaur was a fast runner.

2 Three walking toes spread on the ground for stability as the second leg is lifted.

3 When off the ground, the toes bunched together to minimize air resistance and increase speed.

1 *Albertosaurus* ran with a horizontal back, head held high, and its body balanced by its stiff tail.

① ② ③

## Could a carnivore make a meal of a plant-eater?

A big hunter, such as *Allosaurus*, would have had several advantages over lumbering plant-eater *Stegosaurus*. Not only was *Allosaurus* faster and more quick-witted, but it was also better equipped for killing. *Allosaurus* could slash out with its claws before sinking its razor-sharp teeth into its victim's flesh. *Stegosaurus* might have fought back by swiping out with its tail spikes, but that was unlikely enough to prevent it ending up as food for its killer.

Allosaurus

Stegosaurus

Saurischian hip bones

Strong thigh bone

Vertebra

Muscular tail

Rough scales

Strong leg muscles

Large intestine

Powerful legs

Three-toed feet

## Which dinosaur has the biggest brain?

The dinosaur with the biggest brain was probably *Giganotosaurus*, although this was definitely not the smartest. That honor goes to the troodontid group, which had the biggest brains for their size. These dinosaurs also had large, foward-facing eyes that could focus on prey and may have helped *Troodon* to see at night.

Troodon

## Who hunted the hunters?

It is possible that the big carnivores—*Allosaurus*, *T. rex*, and *Giganotosaurus*—hunted smaller carnivores, such as *Santanaraptor*, as well as herbivorous dinosaurs. These big carnivores were the largest, fiercest animals around, which made them top predators, safe from hunters themselves. Only a severe wound or debilitating illness could have made a big carnivore potential prey.

Santanaraptor

Deinonychus attacking *Tenontosaurus*

# How did hunters kill their prey?

The predatory dinosaurs had to kill to stay alive, and they developed different methods and weapons for efficient hunting. Once they had moved in for the kill, they would have used teeth, claws, and powerful jaws to despatch their victims. Small carnivores generally relied on speed and agility to capture their prey, but when the target was a big dinosaur, such as *Tenontosaurus*, they may have attacked in packs.

**Q** **A** **Did hunters stalk their prey?**
The more intelligent predatory dinosaurs may have stalked their prey, waiting to pounce in a moment of weakness. A lone herbivore, such as this *Iguanodon*, would have been at risk from stalkers such as *Neovenator*. To attack a dinosaur in a herd, the stalker might have separated a weaker animal from the group before moving in for the kill.

*Iguanodon*

Curved claw hooked the prey

Killer claw was flicked forward into victim's flesh

**Q** **A** **Did *Deinonychus* have killer claws?**
This hunter wielded a large, sickle-shaped claw on the second toe of each foot. Experts think that *Deinonychus* held its prey with its hands and jaws and slashed at its victim with one razor-sharp claw until the unfortunate creature was dead.

*Deinonychus* claw

## More Facts

■ *Deinosuchus*, a huge alligator, was capable of feasting on large dinosaurs. This massive, river-dwelling reptile's skull alone measured 6 ft (1.8 m).

■ *Giganotosaurus* may have slammed into its victims to knock them out with its body weight before digging in.

■ Once a big theropod had gorged itself on a kill, smaller predators might move in to strip the bones of flesh.

■ Dinosaurs' teeth survive well as fossils because they are the hardest part of the body and least subject to decay.

■ Marine carnivore *Liopleurodon* may have been able to sniff out potential prey by swimming with its mouth open and "smelling" the water that passed into its nostrils.

Large cavity to house massive jaw muscles

*Allosaurus* skull

Jaws were flexible

*Liopleurodon*

### Q|A What was a killer's main weapon?

The large predator's ultimate weapon was its jaws. They were massive and incredibly powerful. Specially designed "windows" in the skull made it lightweight without losing strength. *Allosaurus*'s jaws were flexible, allowing it to open its mouth wide enough to swallow huge mouthfuls of flesh—perhaps even an entire creature.

### Q|A How were curved fangs used?

Predatory dinosaurs such as *T. rex* had teeth that curved inward. These were designed to give the predator a better grip on its victim. The angle of the teeth prevented an animal from struggling while the daggerlike points pierced its flesh. If a dinosaur lost a tooth in battle or in an accident, a new one grew to replace it.

Curved teeth held prey in place

*Tyrannosaurus* jaw

# Was *T. rex* a scavenger?

With a reputation as the "king of the killers," *Tyrannosaurus rex* was the size of a house, as heavy as an elephant, and had teeth as long and sharp as carving knives. Yet some paleontologists have argued that this fearsome dinosaur was actually a scavenger, feasting only on animals that were already dead. Some of the dinosaur's features appear to be designed for hunting, others for scavenging. The most likely answer is that *T. rex* was both, killing live prey but also feeding on animal remains whenever it found them.

*Tyrannosaurus rex*

Two-fingered hand with sharp claws

Powerful legs

Meat and bones

**Q / A Could tiny arms grapple with prey?**

All tyrannosaurs had small arms but *T. rex*'s were the tiniest for its size. For many years their purpose puzzled paleontologists. However, recent research suggests the arms were handy for hunting. The heavy arm bones, strong muscles, and limited range of movement would have made the arms the right tools for holding struggling prey.

*Tyrannosaurus*

*Ornitholestes*

## Q A How fast was *T. rex*?

Most experts estimate the top speed at between 10–25 mph (16–40 km/h). Studies have shown that *T. rex's* legs weren't strong enough to absorb the pounding of its 6 tons of body weight at faster speeds. However, although *T. rex* was slower than the fastest dinosaurs (such as *Ornitholestes*), it was fast enough to catch potential prey, such as lumbering plant-eater *Triceratops*.

## Q A How big was its bite?

*T. rex* had the biggest and the strongest jaws of any dinosaur—they could measure up to 4 ft (1.2 m) long. Experts estimate that *T. rex* could eat up to 500 lb (230 kg) of meat and bones in a single bite. This is strong evidence that the dinosaur was a hunter, for scavengers would not have needed such size or power.

*Tyrannosaurus rex* jaws

Largest teeth were 9 in (23 cm) long

Hinge for opening lower jaw wide

Field of view overlap

## Q A Do scavengers need a strong sense of smell?

Scavenging animals track down dead meat by following its smell, so a sensitive nose is essential. Experiments have shown that *T. rex* did have a heightened sense of smell—scans of the dinosaur's skull reveal exceptionally large olfactory lobes (smell detectors). But this alone is not enough to prove that it was a scavenger. A good sense of smell is an essential tool for hunting, too.

Field of view of left eye

Field of view of right eye

*T. rex* field of view

Prominent nostrils

## More Facts

■ *Tyrannosaurus rex* would have needed about 300 lb (136 kg) of meat each day to keep it supplied with energy.

■ Scavengers such as vultures and hyenas can digest meat in an advanced stage of decay without getting sick.

■ Some paleontologists think that *T. rex* may have had feathers.

## Q A Did *T. rex* have good eyesight?

Strong vision is essential for hunting but less so for scavenging. *T. rex* had eyes that were angled forward, giving it some degree of binocular vision. This means that it could judge the distance of an object where the fields of view from its left eye and right eye overlapped. *T. rex's* eyesight was probably good enough for stalking prey.

# Did carnivores eat only meat?

Most people think of carnivorous dinosaurs sinking their teeth into a tasty plant-eater, which they certainly did. But they ate other animals, too. Recent evidence suggests that some dinosaurs preferred fish to meat, and others may have eaten both meat and plants. Fish-eating dinosaurs, such as *Suchomimus*, were built a little differently from their meat-eating cousins, with teeth designed for gripping their slippery prey. Dinosaur teeth provide basic information about diet, but paleontologists can discover more details from dinosaurs' fossilized droppings.

Bony ridge along back

Long, narrow jaw with sharp teeth

Strong legs

Suchomimus

Curved thumb claw

## Q How did a dinosaur hook a fish?

A At first, paleontologists were puzzled by *Baryonyx's* long, curved thumb claw. After finding fish near the dinosaur's skeleton, which suggested that it was a fish-eater, they think they know what the dinosaur did with its claw. *Baryonyx* probably used it to hook fish out of the water, in much the same way that bears do.

Baryonyx claw

Claw 12 in (30 cm) long

## More Facts

■ Other fish-eating animals included flying reptile *Dimorphodon*, which swooped down from cliff-sides to snatch up fish.

Dimorphodon

■ All the four-legged dinosaurs were strict herbivores, but two-legged dinosaurs included carnivores, omnivores, and herbivores.

■ A big fish-eating dinosaur such as *Suchomimus* would have to eat a fish 13 ft (4 m) long to satisfy its appetite.

■ Like their closest living reptiles the crocodiles, dinosaurs may have eaten their own young if food was scarce.

## Q A How were fish-eaters like crocodiles?

The long, narrow skulls of fish-eaters were more like the heads of crocodiles than those of other dinosaurs. The jaws were packed with about 100 pointed, serrated teeth. *Spinosaurus* may have dipped its long snout into the shallow waters of a lake or river to search for fish, then crunched them up with its many teeth.

*Nostrils high on snout enabled dinosaur to breathe with its mouth in the water*

*Fish held firm by teeth*

Spinosaurus

## Q A Did any dinosaurs eat mammals?

Carnivores such as *Syntarsus* didn't prey on fellow dinosaurs. Instead, they made do with other animals. Mammals, such as the shrewlike *Megazostrodon* would have made a tasty snack until a more satisfying meal could be found. Many theropods would also have eaten lizards, turtles, and eggs, including those of other dinosaurs.

Syntarsus

Gallimimus

## Q A Were there any dinosaurs that ate both meat and plants?

Most dinosaurs were either carnivores, eating other animals, or herbivores, eating only plants, but a few were able to eat both. The name for these animals is omnivores. Omnivorous dinosaurs were small, birdlike theropods. Omnivore *Gallimimus* darted about the plains, picking off insects and lizards, and also munching on the vegetation.

## Q A How do we know about dinosaur diets?

Fossilized dinosaur droppings, known as coprolites, can reveal valuable information about dinosaur diets. Pieces of bone found in a dropping may belong to another dinosaur or other animal, undigested plant matter may contain identifiable spores or pollen. Paleontologists can even figure out the shape of a dinosaur's intestines from the shape of the coprolite.

Coprolite (dinosaur dung)

# GIANTS OF
THE EARTH

# What is a sauropod?

The most striking characteristic of the sauropods was their size, for they were the biggest animals to walk the Earth. Their body design did not vary as much as in other dinosaur groups—they all had large bodies and small heads, and most had very long necks and tails, like this *Brachiosaurus*. All the sauropods were herbivorous, maintaining their massive bodies with only plant matter. Like their enemies the theropods, the sauropods belonged to the lizard-hipped type of dinosaurs.

Small head

Strong tendon

Big lungs

Shoulder joint

Elbow joint

*Argentinosaurus*

## More Facts

- This infant *Mussaurus* (mouse lizard) is just 7 in (18 cm) long. It belongs to the prosauropod group, once thought to be ancestors of the sauropods.

*Mussaurus*

- In China, the bones of sauropods have been boiled and fed to children for their healing properties,

- The largest land animal today is the African elephant.

### Who was the biggest of them all?

There are several contenders for this title. *Seismosaurus* and *Paralititan* were both giants among sauropods, but *Argentinosaurus* may have been the biggest. Although only a few bones of this dinosaur have been recovered, paleontologists have estimated its length at about 125 ft (37.5 m) and its weight at 80–100 tons. It is still possible that an even bigger sauropod may be discovered.

### What does quadrupedal mean?

A quadrupedal animal, such as *Saltasaurus*, is one that walks on all four legs. All sauropods, and most other plant-eating dinosaurs, were quadrupedal. This was probably because the plant-eaters had large stomachs that tended to pitch their bodies forward onto the front legs, making walking on only the back legs impossible.

Front legs slightly shorter then back legs

*Saltasaurus*

Magyarosaurus

## Were there any small sauropods?

One of the smallest known sauropods measured 20 ft (6 m) from head to tail. *Magyarosaurus* and other smaller sauropods have been discovered in parts of Europe that were a group of islands in Cretaceous times. It is likely that the sauropods living there became smaller over thousands of years because of a limited food supply.

## How long was the longest neck?

The neck of an adult *Mamenchisaurus* was an incredible 46 ft (14 m) long. The neck was made up of 19 spinal bones (vertebrae), more than in any other dinosaur. The vertebrae were linked to one another by bony struts, which made the neck quite stiff. The vertebrae were hollow and thin to make the neck as lightweight as possible.

Mamenchisaurus

Neck held stiffly

Total length of dinosaur was 72 ft (22 m)

Diplodocus

Tail was thick at its base

## Who had the longest tail?

*Diplodocus* is the most likely holder of this title. This dinosaur had a tail measuring around 46 ft (14 m), as long as *Mamenchisaurus's* neck. The tail was composed of about 80 vertebrae, which became narrower at the tail's tip. *Diplodocus* probably used its tail as a counterbalance for its long neck and it may have whipped attackers with its tail, too.

Small intestine

Backbone

Saurischian (lizard) hips

## Did sauropods have thick skin?

Sauropods had thick skin for protection against attackers. However, these skin textures would have varied between groups. A section of fossilized skin from a *Saltasaurus*, above, has been discovered, showing bumpy skin inset with little bony plates. Other sauropods may have had smoother, more lizardlike skin. Some even had ridged spikes running along their backs.

Muscular tail

Large intestine

Strong muscles

Brachiosaurus

Ankle joint

# Was bigger always better?

As tens of millions of years passed, the sauropods and theropods grew ever larger. It seems that they were locked into an evolutionary size race—as the theropods became larger and more fierce, the sauropods grew bigger to counter any attack. In the end, sauropods such as *Camarasaurus* dwarfed *Allosaurus* and the other theropods. Being massive, however, had its disadvantages, such as lack of speed. Meanwhile, other plant-eating dinosaurs developed alternative methods of defense, often growing too tough or too nimble for theropods to tackle.

*Sauropod is 75 ft (3 m) long*

*Camarasaurus*

*Theropod is 39 ft (12m) long*

*Allosaurus*

## Q A Were all the plant-eaters huge?

Not all plant-eating dinosaurs became enormous in response to the threat of theropods. *Gargoyleosaurus* was 10–13 ft (3–4 m) long, one of the smallest of the ankylosaur group. Although relatively small, *Gargoyleosaurus* was capable of surviving an attack by a theropod. Its vicious shoulder spikes and bony back plates would have made it a tough meal.

*Gargoyleosaurus*

## Q A Did sauropods have extra-powerful hearts?

Some experts think that the bigger sauropods, such as *Brachiosaurus*, may have needed large, powerful hearts and super-high blood pressure to pump blood around their massive bodies and up their necks to their brains. It is possible that they had hearts with four chambers, like humans and other mammals, rather than three chambers, like most reptiles.

*Brachiosaurus*

*Heart*

Stiff neck ending
in small head

Strong
leg bones

*Brontopodus*
footprints

## How did sauropods carry their weight?

Experts once thought that sauropods lived in water because they would have been too heavy to support their own weight. Today, they agree that sauropods were designed to carry their weight, just as elephants are. Their legs were as sturdy as pillars and their toes, which splayed out to spread the weight, were cushioned by big pads of flesh. A large fleshy heel helped support the weight.

*Diplodocus*
forefoot

Elephant
forefoot

## Could a plant-eater be quick on its feet?

Not all plant-eaters were big or covered with body armor——some used their agility to escape danger. The ornithopod group of dinosaurs included lightly built animals such as *Dryosaurus*, which could run at high speeds. Like the theropods, *Dryosaurus* had a stiff tail for balancing as it sprinted on its hind legs.

*Dryosaurus*

## What do fossil footprints tell us?

To estimate how fast a dinosaur moved, paleontologists examine the anatomy of the animal and, where available, its footprints. They can figure out its moving speed by measuring distance between the tracks— although footprints from a running dinosaur are very rare. These *Brontopodus* tracks indicate that the large sauropods had a top speed of about 6 mph (10 km/h).

Short arms with
five-fingered
hands

Long, lightly
built legs

## Could *Saltasaurus* rear up on its hind legs?

The skeletons of *Saltasaurus* and some other sauropods suggest that they may have been able to rock back onto their hind legs and lift their front legs off the ground to reach foliage high up in the trees.

1 Slightly longer hind legs meant that the dinosaur's weight could be shifted to the back of the animal.

2 Once on its hind legs, the dinosaur's center of gravity was shifted to the back half of its huge body.

3 The tail acted as a third leg, providing extra stability as the dinosaur balanced on its two hind legs.

①

②

③

# How did plant-eaters find food?

Plants common in the age of the dinosaurs included ginkgo trees, palmlike trees, coniferous trees, and ferns and mosses. It is likely that herbivorous dinosaurs ate all these plants. Different plant-eating dinosaurs developed different ways of breaking down their food. Sauropods, such as *Barosaurus*, raked foliage into their mouths with peglike teeth and swallowed it whole. It was then broken down in their digestive systems. Other plant-eating dinosaurs ground down plant matter with their teeth before swallowing.

*Barosaurus*

Modern-day ginkgo

Fossilized ginkgo

### Q A Were there flowers and grass?

Flowering plants first appeared in the early Cretaceous Period. Passion flowers, as well as flowering trees such as magnolia, beech, oak, maple, and walnut joined earlier plants. It is likely that dinosaurs ate the new flowers alongside leafy plant matter. Recent evidence from dinosaur droppings (coprolites) shows that some sauropods also munched on grass.

Passion flower

### Q A What did sauropods eat?

Their enormous size meant that sauropods had to spend nearly all their time eating just to generate enough energy to stay alive. They probably fed mostly on coniferous trees, steadily munching their way through entire forests. It is this continuous eating that may have created what is known as a "browse line," leaving trees bare of leaves below a certain level.

## Could a plant-eater chew its food?

Plant-eaters didn't have molars, like humans, and many could not chew. But some had toothless, horny beaks for snipping plants, as well as rows of teeth in their cheeks for grinding them down. Each tooth was coarsely serrated. Years of grinding tough plants wore teeth down. Those shown here are from an *Iguanodon*. One is in good condition; the other is worn.

Lower tooth

Worn lower tooth

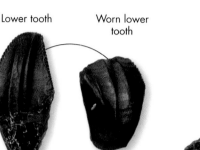

## Were long necks useful?

Some long-necked dinosaurs probably lifted their heads to reach high up in the trees. Others, such as this *Thecodontosaurus*, may also have used them to reach into the middle of low-growing plants. *Thecodontosaurus* was a likely ancestor of the sauropods and had a much shorter neck than its later relatives.

Neck suitable for browsing

Long claws for hooking plants

*Thecodontosaurus*

Cheek teeth for grinding food

*Iguanodon* skull

## More Facts

■ As the plant-eaters' teeth wore down, new ones grew to replace them.

■ Duck-billed dinosaur *Edmontosaurus* had about 1,000 teeth in its cheeks, more than any other dinosaur.

■ Many of the plants that dinosaurs ate, such as ginkgo and ferns, are still common today.

■ Fish-eating sea creature *Elasmosaurus* had a neck 23 ft (7 m) long, half its body length. It probably used this long neck to ambush fish swimming above it.

*Elasmosaurus*

## Did plant-eaters swallow stones?

These smooth stones, known as gastroliths, were recovered from the skeletons of various sauropods. Perhaps the dinosaurs had deliberately swallowed stones to aid their digestion. The stones might have stayed in a dinosaur's digestive system, grinding up the vegetation that it swallowed. However, it is more than likely that raw vegetation was broken down by special bacteria, as happens in the stomachs of cows.

Gastroliths

# Where did plant-eaters live?

*Paralititan*

During the 160 million years that dinosaurs existed, new landmasses appeared and different habitats were created. The herbivores, along with carnivores, lived in most of them, although tropical forest was a favored habitat for big sauropods. Some plant-eaters adapted to extreme conditions, while others may have moved on to find new lands. Whether in a forest or a windswept plain, many of the herbivores spent their lives with each other, perhaps even living in herds of thousands.

## Q/A How had the landscape changed?

By the Cretaceous Period, the world's landmass was splitting into continents, which looked closer to those that we recognize today. New groups of dinosaurs arose in different places. The horned dinosaurs, for example, emerged in Asia, but crossed into North America, where they were able to flourish.

Cretaceous Earth

## Q/A Did some dinosaurs migrate?

Some people think that herds of *Pachyrhinosaurus* used to trek about 2,200 miles (3,500 km) from northern Alaska to Canada each autumn to escape the cold, dark winters. The herds would have returned to Alaska to feed on the lush plants that grew there in the spring.

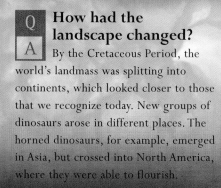

## Did sauropods live together?

**Q** **A** Evidence suggests that many types of plant-eating dinosaurs, including sauropods such as *Barosaurus*, lived together in herds. Being part of a group usually gives an individual animal greater protection against predators. It is also possible that sauropods were sociable animals. A herd may have contained a number of family groups that roamed the countryside together.

*Barosaurus*

*Corythosaurus*

## Who chose to live near swamps?

**Q** **A** Fossils of *Corythosaurus* and other hadrosaurs (sometimes called duck-billed dinosaurs) have been discovered in rocks that were laid down in swamps. People once supposed that the hadrosaurs fed on water plants that grew in swamps, like the modern North American moose. Experts now believe hadrosaurs spent most of their time on dry land.

## More Facts

■ Sauropods were more comfortable in forest habitats because the trees shaded their huge bodies from the Sun.

■ *Leaellynasaura* lived within the Antarctic Circle, where there was little sunlight in winter. Experts believe the dinosaur must have been warm-blooded to survive the dark and cold.

*Leaellynasaura*

■ Among the first dinosaur fossils to be studied were those of the plant-eater *Iguanodon*.

■ All the bird-hipped, or ornithischian, dinosaurs were plant-eaters.

■ In the Cretaceous Period, sauropods declined in North America, but flourished in southern continents.

## Did plant-eaters ever live in trees?

**Q** **A** When fossils of the ornithopod *Hypsilophodon* were discovered in 1849, paleontologists believed that this small plant-eater lived in trees. They thought it used its long tail for balancing while it clung onto branches with its sharp toes. Now experts are convinced that none of the plant-eaters lived in trees, although some of the smaller meat-eaters may have been tree-dwellers.

*Hypsilophodon*

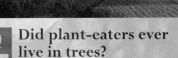

# Methods
## of Defense

# How did plant-eaters fight back?

To defend themselves against predators, the different plant-eating dinosaurs developed an impressive armory of weapons. The ankylosaur *Euoplocephalus* had a ball of thickened bone at the end of its tail, which it could swing at attackers. The stegosaurs had tails studded with daggerlike spikes for stabbing attackers, while the sauropods' size was their main defense. Some dinosaurs had features that puzzle paleontologists, because it is unclear whether they were weapons or merely tools for feeding.

Pointed scutes (bony plates) ran in rows

*Euoplocephalus*

Muscular tail

Thickened bone

Short and broad three-toed feet

*Huayangosaurus*

Long neck

## Q A Could a sauropod crush an attacker?

A big sauropod, such as *Barosaurus*, had one decisive weapon against even the largest theropods—sheer weight. Its 20-ton body could easily crush the bones and suck the air from the lungs of a 3-ton *Allosaurus*. *Barosaurus* may have resorted to crushing attackers in extreme circumstances, such as to protect its young.

*Barosaurus*

Strong, thin tail

## Q A Which dinosaurs had a display of spikes?

A group of dinosaurs called stegosaurs are characterized by their spiked tails and plated backs. *Huayangosaurus* was an early stegosaur, living some 20 million years before its more famous American relative *Stegosaurus*. It may have used its tail spikes to deter attack from larger carnivores.

*Allosaurus*

Flexible armored bands

Protective spikes

Kentrosaurus

Toothless beak

Blunt nails

Sturdy legs

Therizinosaurus

### Q A Which was the spikiest dinosaur?

*Kentrosaurus*, meaning "spiked lizard," was certainly one of the spikiest. It was an East African stegosaur, which measured about 16 ft (5 m) long. Pairs of bone plates protected its neck, shoulders, and back. Six pairs of spikes—each of which was up to 2 ft (60 cm) in length—adorned its lower back and tail. *Kentrosaurus* would have used these spikes to fend off theropods, such as *Allosaurus*.

### Q A Which dinosaur had a thumb spike?

*Iguanodon* was a large herbivore without spines, plates, or claws. Its only defensive weapon was a single long spike on each thumb. Paleontologists believe this dinosaur may have jabbed at attacking theropods with the spike. *Iguanodon* had unusually flexible hands and was able to grasp food in its fingers.

## More Facts

■ *Diplodocus* may have flicked its long tail like a whip, causing serious damage to attackers.

■ Dinosaur fossils often show evidence of fighting in the form of broken bones.

■ Like some dinosaurs, modern iguanas have a row of spikes on their necks and backs to deter attacks from predators.

Land iguana

### Q A How useful were massive claws?

*Therizinosaurus* had three huge, lethal-looking claws on each hand. However, some experts think the claws were too blunt to be used as weapons. Instead, they may have been used for feeding—to pluck foliage from trees or to rip open the nests of termites. If so, how this dinosaur defended itself remains a mystery.

Iguanodon

Thumb spike up to 6 in (15 cm) in length

# Did body armor really help?

Many dinosaurs had some protective armor, but the ankylosaurs were the most heavily armored of all. Some were covered in a mosaic of bony plates and studs, and many bristled with spines and spikes, too. Only their bellies were unprotected, and ankylosaurs may have crouched to avoid exposing them when attacked. It would have taken a hungry theropod to tackle spiky *Gastonia*, which may have responded by driving its shoulder spines into its attacker's leg.

Neck scutes •

*Edmontonia*

## Q A What was the armor made of?

The flat plates embedded in the skin of the ankylosaurs are known as scutes by paleontologists. The ankylosaurs' armor of scutes, studs, and spikes was made of hardened bone, sometimes covered in horn. *Edmontonia* had scutes around its shoulders and along its tail, as well as triangular spikes on its back.

• Curved dorsal spines

• Broad, flat spikes

• Horny, toothless beak

Broad foot    *Gastonia*

Pachycephalosaurus

*Heavy tail*

Hard head

*Powerful legs*

## What was a nasal boss?

One of the horned dinosaurs, *Pachyrhinosaurus*, has a name that means "thick-nosed lizard." On its nose—where its cousins had a sharp horn—*Pachyrhinosaurus* had a big bony knob. This was the nasal boss. Rival family members may have scrapped with each other, using their nasal bosses as weapons.

Pachyrhinosaurus

*Lump of thick bone*

Ankylosaur skin

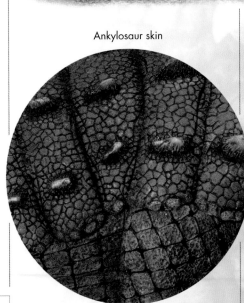

## Which dinosaur is bone-headed?

*Pachycephalosaurus* was an ugly beast. It had a dome-shaped head edged with horny bumps, and several short bony spikes on its nose. The dome was made of solid bone, which was a whopping 10 in (25 cm) thick. *Pachycephalosaurus* may have used its head as a battering ram against attacking predators—or each other.

## Were any sauropods armored?

Although most of the sauropods relied on their size to defend themselves, some of them were lightly armored, too. *Saltasaurus* had two types of armor. Its back and neck were covered in fist-sized bony scutes, and much smaller lumps toughened the skin all over its body.

## More Facts

- Some ankylosaurs were so well-protected they even had bony eyelids.

- Dinosaur remains were first found in Antarctica in 1986, with the discovery of the bulky ankylosaur *Antarctopelta*.

- *Psephoderma* was a marine reptile. Its body was covered in heavy hexagonal plates, like a modern turtle.

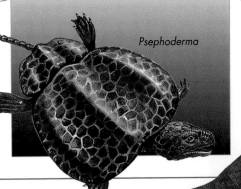

Psephoderma

## Who had bulletproof skin?

Recent research has shown that the skin on the backs and tails of some of the ankylosaurs was virtually bullet-proof—and certainly tooth-proof. The big scutes, smaller irregular plates, and the hexagonal plates interlocked to make the skin so tough and light that experts have likened it to fiberglass.

Saltasaurus

*Smaller lumps*

Bony scutes

*Shorter neck than other sauropods*

# Were frills defensive?

The plated and horned groups of dinosaurs developed some impressive features. They had great frills edged with studs and spikes around their heads, or triangular plates of skin and bone along their backs. Some were used in fighting. But experts believe that some dinosaur features were just for display. Like a peacock's colorful fan of feathers, a male *Pentaceratops*'s head frill may have been used to help it attract a mate.

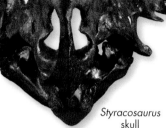

*Styracosaurus* skull

**Q** **Which dinosaur had the spikiest frill?**

**A** *Styracosaurus* was one of the most spectacular looking of the horned dinosaurs. Its head broadened into a large frill that covered the back of its neck. Six long spikes flared from the top of the frill, and the sides were edged with studs. *Styracosaurus* also had a big horn on its snout, but seemingly no horns above its eyes.

Large neck frill

*Pentaceratops*

Plain, bulky body

## Could a skull be a battering ram?

**Q** **A** *Triceratops*, or "three-horned face," had a short nose horn and two long horns above its eyes. Its neck frill was edged with bony studs. About 50 *Triceratops* skulls have been discovered, and many of them show scarring. This is strong evidence that the dinosaur used its tough skull as a weapon against larger predators.

Long spikes

Large nose horn

*Styracosauruses*

Horns

*Triceratops* skull

Eye socket

## Did horned dinosaurs fight each other?

**Q** **A** The horned dinosaurs would have fought off attacking theropods, but they probably also clashed with each other. They may have crashed their heads together, damaging each other's frills with their horns and spikes, or locked horns and shoved. Such battles would have been fought over territory or potential mates.

Arched back

Large, bony plates

Sharp tail

Heavy build

*Stegosaurus*

## More Facts

- The plant-eating dinosaur *Protoceratops* had a neck frill, but the males had much bigger frills than the females. This supports the idea that frills attracted females.

- The head of *Styracosaurus* was taller than an average-sized man!

- Some dinosaurs, including *Stegoceras*, had bony thickenings on their skulls. They were too fragile to provide self-defense and were probably used to attract mates.

*Stegoceras*

## Which dinosaur had a main sail?

**Q** **A** The big carnivore *Spinosaurus* had spines up to 6 ft (2 m) long along its back. These were connected by skin, making the feature look like a sail. This sail may have helped *Spinosaurus* keep cool in the hot African climate, or simply been used for display—to attract a mate.

## What were *Stegosaurus*'s plates for?

**Q** **A** The bony plates running along *Stegosaurus*'s back were almost certainly not weapons. Experts think they were covered in skin, making them quite soft, with blood vessels (veins) inside. If this is correct, the plates may have helped to regulate body temperature. They would have absorbed the Sun's heat, warming up *Stegosaurus*.

*Spinosaurus*

# How did dinosaurs escape danger?

When threatened, animals will try to avoid a fight, and dinosaurs probably behaved much like other animals. *Gallimimus* was one of the fastest dinosaurs, possibly sprinting at speeds of up to 50 mph (80 km/h) to outrun predators. Other dinosaurs found different ways to keep out of harm's way. Some developed skin that was colored and patterned to blend in with their environments. Others kept to the safety of the herd. A few dinosaurs could even make sounds that signaled the approach of danger.

*Gallimimus*

Flexible neck

Tube of nasal bones

*Parasaurolophus*

### Q A How did dinosaurs sound out a warning?

Duck-billed dinosaur *Parasaurolophus* may have used its skull to communicate with other dinosaurs. The unusual crest on this dinosaur's head consisted of tubes connected to its nostrils. By blowing through its crest and nose, *Parasaurolophus* could have made a trumpeting noise, perhaps to warn that predators were nearby.

Claws on wing

### Q A Could any dinosaurs fly away?

Dinosaurs are usually described as land animals, but one species became so birdlike that it was able to fly. Experts are not sure whether to describe *Archaeopteryx* as a bird or a dinosaur. It was certainly capable of flying from danger, but unlike modern birds it had teeth, a bony tail, and clawed wings.

## Was there safety in numbers?

**Q** **A** Dinosaurs living in herds would probably have been much safer than those that lived alone. If a herd of *Triceratops* was being stalked by a predator, for example, the adults could threaten to charge, while keeping their young well inside the group. *Triceratops* may also have been able to run at speeds of 15 mph (25 km/h).

Triceratops

Long tail for balance while running

Birdlike beak

## More Facts

- The fossil remains of the tiny dinosaur, *Microraptor*, were first described in 2000. It could climb trees and possibly escape danger by gliding through the air from branch to branch.

- Desert hunter *Herrerasaurus* may have had a sandy-colored skin with irregular stripes to stop it standing out in the barren landscape.

Herrerasaurus

- Fossil evidence shows that some dinosaurs lived in groups. This includes fossils of the same dinosaur species found together, the fossilized trackways of dinosaurs traveling in herds, and groups of fossilized nests.

## Did dinosaurs use camouflage?

**Q** **A** No one can know for sure whether dinosaurs were plain or patterned, because color fades away quickly and skin decomposes soon after death. However, it is highly likely that many dinosaurs would have skin colors and patterns that helped them to merge with their environment. A dinosaur living in scrubland, such as *Velociraptor*, may have been any one of a variety of colors.

Feathers attached to bony tail

Archaeopteryx

Lightly built body

Long wing feathers typical of flying birds

Tiger stripes

Velociraptor

Green and lizardlike

Spotty skin pattern

# END OF AN ERA

# What killed the dinosaurs?

Some 65 million years ago, a catastrophic event occurred that wiped out more than half of all life on Earth, including the dinosaurs. Most experts believe this mass extinction was caused by an enormous asteroid crashing into the Earth. So much dust was blasted into the atmosphere that day became night for months on end and the temperatures plummeted. Close to the impact site the landscape was devastated, and dying dinosaurs would have stumbled around looking in vain for food and shelter.

*Triceratops* was one of the last survivors

### Q A What is an asteroid?

An asteroid is a rocky object—smaller than a planet—that orbits the Sun. Every so often, their orbits bring some asteroids crashing into the Earth's surface. Although most are too small to cause long-term damage, the massive asteroid that probably caused the Cretaceous mass extinction made a crater 112 miles (180 km) wide.

Asteroid impact

### Q A What else might have happened?

No one can be sure that an asteroid collision alone was the cause of the dinosaurs' extinction. Scientists also think that at the end of the Cretaceous Period there were numerous volcanic eruptions in India. These might have polluted the atmosphere with so much dust that the Sun's rays could not penetrate, and many creatures may have died of cold.

Erupting volcano

*Tyrannosaurus rex*

*Pterodactylus*

*Mosasaurus*

**Q A Did flying reptiles all die?**

Throughout the time of the dinosaurs, the skies were filled with flying reptiles, but no pterosaurs survived the mass extinction. Reptiles would never take to the skies again and no human would see a *Pterodactylus* or a *Quetzalcoatlus*, the largest flying animal ever, swooping overhead.

**Q A What happend to marine animals?**

When seas still teemed with life, the most dominant groups of sea creatures were the dinosaurs' distant relatives, marine reptiles. Like the dinosaurs, the marine reptiles, such as *Mosasaurus*, were all killed in the extinction event. Many other sea creatures died out or were seriously diminished, although fish were mostly unaffected.

## More Facts

■ One early theory suggested that the dinosaurs' extinction was caused by mammals eating all their eggs.

*Ichthyornis*

■ Many of the early birds, such as this *Ichthyornis*, became extinct, although others survived.

■ A study of leaf fossils in North Dakota showed that 85 percent of plants there vanished at the end of the Cretaceous Period.

■ Sea crocodiles died out, but river crocodiles continued life as normal.

**Q A Which meat-eaters were the last survivors?**

The big theropod *T. rex* was among the last meat-eating dinosaurs to walk the Earth. After the asteroid impact, dead and dying animals would have been plentiful, so it is unlikely *T. rex* died of hunger. It is possible that, together with other dinosaurs, *T. rex* died out because the low temperatures made all hatchlings female.

**Q A Which plant-eaters survived to the end?**

The ankylosaurs were some of the last herbivorous dinosaurs. It is possible that smaller plant-eaters close to the spot where the asteroid hit escaped harm by burrowing into the ground. In the long term, these plant-eaters would have gone hungry because many plants were damaged or destroyed by the lack of light and heat.

*Ankylosaurus*

# Who was top predator after *T. rex*?

It was millions of years before big animals reappeared following the mass extinction. While the dinosaurs were alive, mammals remained relatively small, but they gradually evolved to replace dinosaurs as the dominant land animals. Hoofed beast *Andrewsarchus* became the biggest carnivorous land mammal ever. However, these large mammals faced competition from an unlikely source when birds also evolved into fierce predators.

**Q A** **What did predatory mammals eat?**

*Andrewsarchus* would have been able to hunt down plant-eating mammals, resembling this early hoofed herbivore called *Phenacodus*. About the size of a sheep, *Phenacodus* was lightly built so it stood some chance of escaping a predator. It probably lived in herds and kept to forests for feeding and shelter.

*Phenacodus*

Heavy body covered in dense fur

*Andrewsarchus*

Powerful jaw muscles

Huge canine teeth for crunching through bone

Toes tipped with short hooves

*Uintatherium*

**Q A** **When did big plant-eaters reappear?**

Some 20 million years after the mass extinction, big plant-eating animals were back on the scene. *Uintatherium* was about the size and shape of a rhinoceros and had pillarlike, weight-bearing legs. It had three pairs of horns on its head and tusklike canine teeth, which it probably used for fighting. *Uintatherium* lived on a diet of leaves and fruit.

_Thick, long tail_

**Q A** Ten million years after the disappearance of the pterosaurs, the first flying mammals appeared. Bats have changed little since then and are still the only flying mammals. Many bats are nocturnal and use their special sense of hearing to find their way and locate prey in the dark.

_Large ears for hearing high-frequency sounds_

_Icaronycteris_

_Strong limbs to support its heavy weight_

_Ambulocetus_

## More Facts

■ Many bird groups evolved, including modern ones, such as owls, swifts, herons, and eagles.

■ Early penguins included some giant forms that grew up to 5 ft (1.5 m) tall.

■ Fossil records show that ferns were the first plants to return after the mass extinction.

_Tree fern_

## Did early mammals live in water?

**Q A** This animal looks like an otter, but was, in fact, a very early whale. Although _Ambulocetus_ could walk on dry land, it was also a powerful swimmer, showing how whales evolved from land-dwelling mammals. It would take about 10 million years before watery mammals, such as _Ambulocetus,_ evolved into the whales that we recognize today.

## Which birds were predators?

**Q A** Large, carnivorous, flightless birds became some of the world's fiercest predators. _Titanis,_ or "terror bird," was about 7 ft (2 m) tall and had a sharp, hooked beak and huge claws. _Titanis_ hunted small mammals on North America's open plains, where it competed with the big carnivorous mammals to be top predator.

_Massive beak for tearing flesh_

_Titanis_

_Claws for seizing prey_

Crocodile

# Which animals are as old as dinosaurs?

Even though dinosaurs were around for 160 million years, other animals have survived for as long, or even longer. Ancient animals live everywhere—on land, in the sky, and in the seas and rivers. Many of them have changed little from their prehistoric forms—crocodilians have not needed to adapt since Cretaceous times. If their habitats are preserved, these animals could continue living for millions more years.

*Delicate wings strengthened by fine veins*

Dragonfly

**Q** **Did any land reptiles survive the extinction?**
**A** Small lizards lived throughout the Mesozoic Era, and they are still with us today. Paleontologists are not sure why these reptiles were unaffected by whatever killed the dinosaurs. It is possible that when many plants had died lizards burrowed into the ground and hibernated to escape the hazardous surface conditions.

*Heavily armored skin*

**Q** **Which are the most successful animals?**
**A** Insects are the most numerous and diverse animals that have ever existed on Earth. There are millions of different insect species and some of them have existed, relatively unchanged, since before the time of the dinosaurs. The oldest dragonfly fossil ever found is about 320 million years old, and dragonflies are still a common sight today.

Iguana

*Feet designed for running on land*

*Scaly skin typical of lizards*

*Venom is injected from the tail*

Cockroach

*Tough shell protects soft body parts*

*Short, sturdy limbs*

Scorpion

## Q A How ancient are arachnids?

Fossil evidence suggests that arachnids—the animal group that includes spiders and scorpions—are more than 400 million years old. There are hundreds of thousands of species today. All of them are predators, killing by injecting deadly chemicals, called venom, into their prey. The venom of some scorpions can kill humans.

## Q A Are cockroaches indestructible?

Cockroaches could be the most hardy of all insects. They eat almost anything, but they can also survive without food for about a month. They can even recover after being frozen. Cockroaches live everywhere except the polar regions. They have existed for 300 million years.

*Broad, powerful jaw*

## Q A Which are the oldest sea creatures?

Marine invertebrates (animals without backbones), including clams and jellyfish, are the oldest. However, the most ancient big sea animal is undoubtedly the shark. These formidable fish have survived more than 400 million years of history, including the Cretaceous extinction.

Great white shark

## What is a crocodilian?

This is the name for a group of archosaurs made up of crocodiles and their relatives. The first crocodilians appeared about the same time as the dinosaurs and lived on land. Soon, they evolved to live in seas and rivers. Today, there are 23 crocodilian species.

1 *Geosaurus was an aquatic crocodilian of the Jurassic Period. Instead of the heavy armor that most crocodilians have, Geosaurus had smooth skin, making it a more agile swimmer than its relatives.*

*Geosaurus*

*Deinosuchus*

2 *At about 50 ft (15 m) in length, Deinosuchus was one of the biggest crocodilians. Its powerful jaws could probably crush a large dinosaur.*

# Are birds related to dinosaurs?

A heron may not look like a dinosaur, but striking similarities exist between birds and dinosaurs. In recent years, new evidence has confirmed the link between them. Dinosaur fossils have been found that prove some species had distinctly birdlike features, and bird fossils have shown that the earliest birds had dinosaurlike attributes, too. Paleontologists think that a particular group of dinosaurs evolved into the thousands of bird species that exist today. Though we will never see a living dinosaur, we can see their descendants in the skies above us.

Keen eyes to spot prey

Slender head

Jaw lined with sharp teeth

Stiff tail

*Compsognathus*

## Q&A: How are dinosaur and bird bones similar?

Like birds, many dinosaurs had lightweight bones. Most animals have sturdy bones, but the bones of some dinosaurs and pterosaurs contained air-filled cavities to lessen the creature's weight. This was a vital asset for flying. There is another remarkable similarity—the skeletons of early birds and some theropods are almost identical.

## Q&A: Which dinosaurs do birds come from?

Paleontologists think birds evolved from a group of small, nimble, carnivorous theropods called maniraptorans. Members of this group, such as *Compsognathus*, are characterized by several birdlike features, including long legs and feet. Most importantly, they seized prey with arms that worked very much like wings.

Lightweight bird bone

## More Facts

■ In the far distant past only about one bird species became extinct every century, but today the rate is about 100 times that.

■ This fossil of the feathered carnivore *Archaeopteryx* (meaning "ancient wing") was discovered in 1861, and was later bought by a German museum.

*Archaeopteryx* fossil remains

■ The smallest dinosaur relative in the sky today is the bee hummingbird of Cuba, which weighs just 0.07 oz (1.95 g).

## When did the first true bird appear?

*Confuciusornis* was the first known bird to have a horny toothless beak, like modern birds, although it still had dinosaurlike claws on its wing feathers. It appeared in Cretaceous China about 120 million years ago. Experts believe it had a different flying technique from that of birds today. Its large toes suggest that it could probably walk and climb, too.

Hooked point at end of bill

Dodo

Claws attached to wings

Confuciusornis

Tiny, flightless wings

Warm feathers covering body

## Which dinosaur looks like a bird?

When its fossil was discovered in 1998, experts debated whether *Shuvuuia* was a birdlike dinosaur or a dinosaurlike bird. Despite its birdlike features, including a coat of downy feathers, most paleontologists identified *Shuvuuia* as a member of a distinct group of theropod dinosaurs, characterized by their short, powerful arms. *Shuvuuia* may have used its arms to rip open termite nests.

## Why have so many bird species died out?

There are fewer than 10,000 bird species in the world today, but other species existed according to fossil records. Most of these died out naturally, but more recently, birds have become extinct because of human activities. In the 17th century, the flightless dodo was one of the first birds to die out because of hunting and the introduction of other predators, such as pigs. Loss of habitat is another main reason that birds become extinct.

Heron

Insect preserved in amber

Body shape similar to a modern bird

Long legs for fast running

## Could dinosaurs ever return?

In the 1993 film *Jurassic Park*, experts brought dinosaurs back to life with dinosaur DNA taken from the body of a mosquito preserved in amber. In reality, any dinosaur DNA would almost certainly be too small a sample and too broken up to recreate a dinosaur. However, technology is always improving and dinosaur fossils are still being discovered...

Three-toed clawed feet

Shuvuuia

# INDEX

# CREDITS

The publisher would like to thank the following for their kind permission to reproduce their photographs:

Key: a=above; b=below/bottom; c=center; l=left; r=right; t=top.

**Alamy Images:** Mediacolor's 38t (b/g); Natural History Museum, London 59tr. **Corbis:** Gunter Marx Photography 30-31 (b/g); Wolfgang Kaehler 19cra; William Manning 27clb; Alfio Scigliano/Sygma 52bl. **DK Images:** American Museum of Natural History 42bc, 46tr; Bedrock Studios 10-11, 14-15t, 17br, 34-35, 35c, 55br, 55cra;

Robert L. Braun—modelmaker 6tl, 7b, 14br (stegosaurus), 14cr, 44-45c, 47c, 47tr, 58cl; Centaur Studios—modelmakers 15bl (baryonyx), 43br; Jonathan Hately—modelmaker 28t; Graham High at Centaur Studios—modelmaker 4, 7t, 13br, 15fbr (triceratops), 26tl, 27br, 27tl; 48ftr, 48tr, 48-49tc, 49ftl, 49tl; Jeremy Hunt at Centaur Studios—modelmaker 6bl, 10c, 36l; Museo Arentino De Cirendas Naterales, Buenos Aires 32tr, 33cr; Natural History Museum, London 5, 12br, 13cr, 19tr, 22tl, 23bc, 25br, 33ca, 39br, 45c, 47cla; Peabody Museum of Natural History, Yale University 24bc; Royal Tyrell Museum 44tr; Gary Staab—modelmaker 6-7; State Museum of Nature, Stuttgart 12-13, 19cla, 25cl; Dennis Wilson—Staab Studios 46bl, 46br; Jerry Young 56-57c. **Getty Images:** Science Faction/Louie Psihoyos 35cla. **Natural Visions:** Richard Coomber/Heather Angel 48-49c (b/g). **Natural History Museum,**

**London:** 13clb. naturepl.com: Pete Oxford 58-59. **Science Photo Library:** David A. Hardy, Futures: 50 Years In Space 52cra; S. R. Maglione 46b (b/g).

**Jacket images: Front: Corbis:** Charles Platiau/Reuters. **Back: DK Images:** Bedrock Studios ftl; Jonathan Hateley- modelmaker bl; Natural History Museum, London fclb. **Spine: DK Images:** Robert L. Braun—modelmaker cb (Compsognathus).

All other images © Dorling Kindersley
For further information see: www.dkimages.com

**Dorling Kindersley** would also like to thank Jenny Finch and Andrea Mills for their editorial help; Lynn Bresler for the index; Johnny Pau, Marilou Prokopiou, and Duncan Shotton for design assistance.